Library of
Davidson College

EUROPE AND MONEY

By the same author

THE SOCIAL ECONOMY OF FRANCE
EUROPEAN MONETARY INTEGRATION *(with John R. Presley)*
THE WORLD MONETARY CRISIS
THE EXTERNAL ECONOMIC RELATIONS OF THE EEC

EUROPE AND MONEY

Peter Coffey
Senior Research Fellow and Head of the Economics Section
Europa Institut, University of Amsterdam

HOLMES & MEIER PUBLISHERS, INC.
IMPORT DIVISION
IUB Building
30 Irving Place, New York, N.Y. 10003

© Peter Coffey 1977

All rights reserved. No part of this publication may be reproduced or transmitted, in any form or by any means, without permission

First published 1977 by
THE MACMILLAN PRESS LTD
London and Basingstoke
Associated companies in New York
Dublin Melbourne Johannesburg and Madras

ISBN 0 333 21404 8

Printed in Great Britain by
THE BOWERING PRESS LTD
Plymouth

This book is sold subject to the standard conditions of the Net Book Agreement

Contents

	Preface	7
1	The World Monetary and Economic Order	11
2	The Theory of Integration and Western Europe	23
3	Optimum Currency Area: Theories Re-examined	41
4	Towards a Monetary Union	60
5	Europe and Money: the Future	77
	Notes	87
	Index	91

Preface

The initiative for embarking upon this study came as a result of an invitation to the author from the Economics Faculty of the University of Amsterdam to give a special programme of lectures on 'European Economic and Monetary Union' in the first months of 1976. Although only a small amount of the material given in those lectures is used here, they nevertheless encouraged the author to re-examine certain facets of the theory of economic integration and the evolution of the European Economic Community from a wider and more practical standpoint, including where possible welfare concepts.

In the first chapter the world economic and monetary order as it existed up to the outbreak of the First World War is examined and compared with the situation that we have known since 1945. The purpose of this background survey is to put the evolving national principles of economic and monetary policy in a wider context. In the second chapter a survey of the theory of economic integration is made and its relevance to the European Economic Community is assessed. Here the author maintains that it was the national economic policy as applied in West Germany and France in the 1950s which left a greater mark on the Community, rather than the conventional economic integration theory. Readers are asked to excuse the author's omission of a specific reference to free trade area theories; this was not through any lack of respect for such theories, but simply because this study is mainly concerned with the Common Market. However, the author would point out that he considers that some economically weaker European countries could obtain greater economic welfare benefits through special free trade agreements with the Common Market than through full membership of the organisation.

The third chapter of the work is devoted to a re-examination of optimum currency area theories, and in Chapter 4 the progress made towards an economic and monetary union is analysed; suggestions are made regarding various ways in which this union might be achieved.

In the last chapter the author looks towards the future of 'Europe and money' and again makes suggestions regarding possible policy choices. The book closes on a somewhat optimistic tone, since the author discerns the beginnings of rediscovery of the principle of monetary discipline by some European countries, and this, he maintains, presages a convergence of national monetary policies. With the eventual adoption by the Council of Ministers of the draft European Company Law and of the proposals to harmonise banking legislation, the author forecasts a greater inter-penetration of the field of services in the European Economic Community and therefore a further increase in consumer welfare. Finally, he calls for the creation of a European employment/investment agency and an attempt to narrow the gap, in some cases, a glaring one, between Europe's rich and poor.

The author is grateful to Martin Goedings for his careful preparation of Table 2, showing Europe's foreign investments. He also wishes to thank Misses Mensing, Moolhuysen and Schönhuth for assistance with the typing of this text.

P.C.

Amsterdam
August 1976

1 The World Monetary and Economic Order

THE NINETEENTH-CENTURY BACKGROUND

Europe's painful moves towards economic and monetary integration are encouraging Europeans to look back to the nineteenth century and to the period immediately preceding the First World War in an attempt to find solutions to present problems. Whether or not we shall find remedies for present ills is not the only reason for examining this period. Without such an examination it would be very difficult for us to understand our present state of economic development and the different attitudes towards economic and monetary integration.

Then, as now, nations were at different stages of economic development. This fact tended to influence the attitude of European nations towards free trade. The United Kingdom, which had been the precursor of the industrial revolution, favoured the theories of Smith and Ricardo on free trade; Germany and other countries however were still in the process of building their industries and thus supported the theories of

List. Furthermore, in contrast with Britain, continental countries wished to protect their agriculture.

Normally speaking these facts should have reduced trade, but, as Maddison and Kuznets[1] have observed, with the outbreak of the First World War we had witnessed an explosion in the growth of world trade. This was probably due in part to the gradual adoption of free trade principles. To this evolution should be added other factors such as technical innovation (particularly transport developments), international capital flows and, possibly, the use of the gold standard.

Certainly it would have been very difficult for persistent growth in world trade to have developed without the existence of some satisfactory international monetary system. A balance had to be maintained, then as now, between growth and inflation. The means of achieving this balanced system was apparently found in the adoption of the gold standard.

At the outset it should be stressed that the gold standard meant different things to different countries. Its origins are to be found in Peel's Bank Act of 1844, whereby the central bank (in this case, the Bank of England) aimed at preventing inflation caused by excessive lending via a strict control of the note issue. Hence any increase in the note issue, beyond a limited amount issued against government stock, had to bear a one-to-one relationship in gold kept in the vaults of the central bank. This was the basis of the gold standard which was gradually adopted by other countries during the course of the nineteenth century.

The actual working of the mechanism of the gold standard at an international level was intended to be simple and effective. Against a background of gold backing for the note issue and convertibility, any balance of payments deficit would result in an outflow of gold, a contraction in the monetary supply and a resultant increase in the price of money (credit). In the case of a balance of payments surplus, the reverse process would result. Such were the observations made by the Cunliffe Committee in 1919.[2]

It is possible that the existence of the gold standard did provide the European and world trading and monetary systems with a basic discipline. But, it is also certain that the gold standard meant different things to different countries and that other considerations helped the system to function satisfactorily.

During the nineteenth century three great European financial centres developed. These were Berlin, London and Paris. Berlin tended to apply a strict gold standard internally and, probably for strategic purposes, to defend its gold reserves. London was the world's free gold market. However London did not, despite the existence of Peel's Bank Act, respect the rigidities of the gold standard as did Berlin. The Bank Act did not cover cheque issue, a major part of world trade was carried out in sterling, and Britain's deficits with the United States and continental Europe were heavily cushioned by surpluses with the colonies – and in particular with India.

Paris came closest to the example of Berlin in its adoption of the gold standard, the major difference being that Paris was the world's final gold reserve and was always willing to help London and, indirectly, New York.[3]

All these great European financial centres floated international loans of different periods of duration and all received deposits from foreign governments. They also tended to reinvest these deposits internationally and to invest their balance of payments surpluses.[4] This situation has led some economists to talk of a 'good creditor policy'. Keynes hoped in some way to recreate this system – without its defects – after the Second World War.

Apart from the purely technical and political considerations just mentioned, certain specific features developed from 1870 until the outbreak of the First World War. With the signing of the trade agreement between Britain and France, there was a definite move towards free trade. An enormous upsurge can be noted in the last part of the nineteenth century and the early part of the present century in the overseas investments of Britain, France and Germany. In the case of the United Kingdom, as Figure 1 shows, the financial adjustment depended on the artificial financial surplus which Britain enjoyed *vis-à-vis* India. Further, what this figure does not show is that a major part of Britain's investments and trade was transacted within the Empire, with the United States and with Latin America.

With regard to the great European overseas investments, the fundamental questions which have never been adequately put nor clearly answered are, what were the real motives for such an outflow and what, if any, welfare considerations were involved? Was

The World Monetary and Economic Order

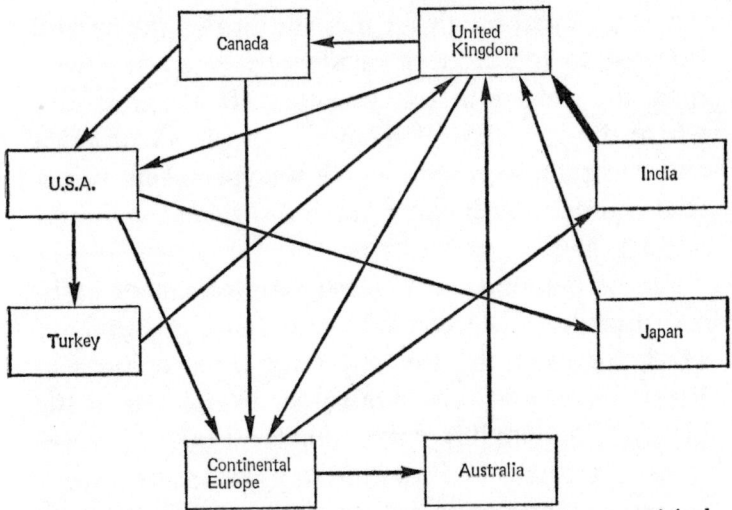

International financial compensation 1890–1914 (based on an original diagram by S. B. Saul)

profitability the only maxim involved? Were colonial considerations the only factors which influenced investment decisions?

The complete answers to these questions are unlikely ever to be known; and it is probable that the motives were mixed. Whenever European colonial powers invested in their colonies, the motives were fairly clear. They usually enjoyed monopoly in these territories and could expect handsome profits from their investments. Many economists have assumed that also important was the finding of markets for European products. One must presume that most overseas investments were made because they were assumed at least to be profitable – either financially and/or politically. However, when one attempts to regard welfare considerations the ground is much less firm. Some economists and politicians believed in the beneficial effects (through an increase in the choice and decrease in the price of goods) of free trade – here, then, the welfare motive was clear. It was clear also where the agricultural territories of North America and Australia were developed, thus providing industrial countries with cheap food. But there the matter seems to end.

It is certain that some investments were made without prior careful economic and financial analysis. Thus, for example, the important French loans to Russia were politically motivated. In the case of the United Kingdom it is certain that some of the finances invested in the colonies would have been better used, in terms of economic and welfare considerations in Britain's own domestic industry. The catastrophic results of this lack of foresight are still being felt by Britain to the present day. These considerations might lead us to judge the benefits of the world economic and monetary structure between 1870 and 1913 to have been somewhat mixed. On the one hand, while different countries tended domestically to interpret the gold standard in different ways, they did obey the fundamental international maxim of the gold standard as demonstrated by fixed exchange rates and convertibility. However, these differences in the interpretation and application of the gold standard at a domestic level, plus the considerations of priority given to the direction of overseas investment, did involve serious preferences by the public authorities, not dissimilar perhaps to the preference for financial support for the agricultural sector in the European Economic Community. Thus, for example, while the outflow of capital from the United Kingdom was subject to minimal control by the public authorities, the French Government influenced the political direction of loans which resulted in the important loans to Russia (as noted above), and the German authorities insisted on priority being given to domestic industry in the capital market. When domestic needs had been satisfied, investment outside Germany was made according to national interests. One of these interests was the military strengthening of Germany's allies.

My observation is that in all the cases under consideration the population of the European countries which were investing overseas tended to lose in welfare terms. The only exceptions tended to be the already mentioned case of investment in overseas agricultural areas and Germany's insistence on the necessity of giving priority to domestic investment. Both Britain and France should have taken a leaf out of Germany's book. In the case of loans which were made for purely political ends, the economic result was a total loss. Some economists would tend to stress the importance of the markets which were created through overseas investment. This was certainly true where agriculture and the development of railways were concerned, but where these developments took place within an empire the investor was condemned, in the long run, to some degree of economic sclerosis.

THE NINETEENTH CENTURY AND THE PRESENT TIME

A fairly clear picture emerges from this brief survey. Towards the latter part of the nineteenth century,

18 *Europe and Money*

three major financial centres had arisen in Western Europe. Each of these centres adhered to the gold standard – which for international monetary purposes mainly meant the maintenance of fixed exchange rates. All three centres were the capitals of a colonial empire and they owned considerable overseas investments. Likewise they were greatly increasing their overseas trade. There existed also a willingness on the part of two centres, London and Paris, to help each other in times of financial stress – and to help New York, since the United States did not at that time possess a developed money market.

This picture naturally leads to a number of questions. The increase in overseas investment and trade which has been noted immediately suggests a form of international division of labour. This was particularly so in the case of the United Kingdom and her colonies. Again, this fact leads one to ask whether the existence of the international gold standard, international investment and trade until 1913, at least in the case of the United Kingdom, essentially presupposed colonialism. A number of writers (in particular de Cecco)[5] have answered this question in the affirmative. Such a situation would also tend to underline what has already been mentioned – that the different financial centres of Europe tended to specialise in different kinds of international business – a fact which has tended to influence their activities down to the present day.

However, three key observations should be borne in mind when transposing the European situation from the period before 1913 to that which we have known since the mid- and late-1950s. The three observations, which are as valid today as they were before 1913, are that Western Europe remains the key trading bloc of the world; that until relatively recently, Europe depended upon an international division of labour whereby the Third World tended to supply raw materials, energy, semi-manufactures and, in some cases, agricultural products, in exchange for the more sophisticated industrialised products of Europe; and that now, as then, Europe is one of the greatest sources of international investment. All these facts tend to heighten the importance of Europe when considering basic principles of international economic and/or monetary integration.

One major difference between the period which existed until 1913 and the post-1945 situation and later the post-1973 situation, is that whereas in the former period the European financial centres had only occasionally temporary recourse to intra-European monetary assistance, during the latter period (especially in the case of Britain) such assistance has been a much more common occurrence. Nor had this aid been restricted to intra-European sources. Further, although some direct capital investment did take place among the European countries before 1913, investment in European countries from non-European sources was almost non-existent. Also Europe was, at that time, a massive exporter of capital at an international level.

Since 1945, and particularly after 1958 and again after 1973, the situation has radically altered. Although Western Europe remains a net exporter[6] of capital, she has nevertheless been an important recipient of capital. After the Second World War, this was inevitable. With the formation of the European Economic Community, however, there was a sudden inflow of capital from non-member countries – and especially from the United States. Following the oil/energy crisis, some European countries actively encouraged the inflow of capital from both European and non-European sources. This last occurrence, while marking a change in capital flows, also indicates a rather dramatic change in the international division of labour. Equally it could presage a greater degree of self-reliance on energy production by the Europeans themselves.

A further major difference between the two periods is that while in the former period economic and trade relations were conducted on a strictly state-to-state basis, with each state following individualistic economic and trading policies, the latter period is notable for the development of international organisations and agreements (the IMF, the IBRD and the GATT) and of important regional economic groupings. Thus although the differences which marked the economic evolution of individual countries (especially France, Germany and the United Kingdom) in the nineteenth century do continue to influence the current policies and performance of these countries, such influences begin to pervade a much larger area – in the present case, the European Economic Community. While international relations tended to be undertaken on a bilateral basis in the former period, there is now a growing tendency for countries to act as a group. The best, most recent example of this has been the conclusion of the Lomé Agreement between the Common Market and the ACP countries.

At a strictly monetary and welfare level the problem, both theoretical and practical, for the European Economic Community is one of balance. For example, what are the best welfare conditions for linking parities of currencies or for allowing floating? What is the optimum welfare balance between interpenetration within the Community and a united employment policy? What degree of free trade can the Common Market afford *vis-à-vis* third parties? To what degree should the Community control investment by third parties in the Common Market? The options and the overall situation are at the same time both more com-

Net Foreign Investments of EEC member countries (1969–74) in US $m

		1969	1970	1971	1972	1973	1974
1	Belgium*	262	162	267	233	529	698
2	Denmark	109	75	80	87	95	96
3	France	102	249	129	93	251	795
4	Germany	−191	−263	158	148	384	649
5	Ireland	N.A.	N.A.	N.A.	N.A.	N.A.	N.A.
6	Italy	135	496	121	410	370	397
7	Netherlands	−90	18	135	−85	47	−601
8	U.K.	−553	−461	−567	−877	−2308	−1819
	U.S.A.	−4531	−3251	−4913	−3152	−2327	−5230
	Japan	−134	−261	−151	−555	−1947	−1811

Source: IFS, xxix, no. 3 (Mar 1976) IMF, Washington, D.C.
* Including Luxemburg.
Notes:
A *minus sign* indicates a debit entry on the balance of payments' capital account. Assets have been purchased from foreigners.
Other figures indicate a credit entry on the balance of payments' capital account. Assets have been sold to foreigners.
N.A. = not availabe.

plex and more clear than those which existed before the First World War.

The crisis which Europe has undergone since 1973 has tended also to re-activate the old European financial centres and to underline their international specialisation. It has heralded the beginning of a profound change between Europe and the Third World and in the whole of the external economic and monetary relations of the Common Market.[7] The changed situation is also leading individual European countries to re-examine and to change their national economic and monetary management and philosophy. Last, but not least, the profound changes which Europe is now experiencing provide a golden opportunity for a re-examination of the basic principles of economic integration, both at a strictly European level as well as in a wider international context.

2 The Theory of Integration and Western Europe

In the first chapter some emphasis was placed on the supposed workings of the gold standard and the attitude of some nations towards free trade and towards protectionism; particular emphasis was placed on the important role of Western Europe as a source of international capital investment. According to the statistics of the League of Nations for 1913, the total gross long-term investments made by Western Europe amounted to 40·5 billion dollars. The main capital-exporting countries were the United Kingdom ($18 billion), France ($9 billion) and Germany ($5·8 billion). The United Kingdom, during the years 1910–13, was exporting capital each year which was the equivalent of ten per cent of her gross national product. It seemed, therefore, that when the First World War broke out Western Europe was economically particularly strong. As has already been indicated, during the occasional temporary crises which occurred in one or another financial centre (especially the Baring crisis in 1890 and the New York crisis in

24 Europe and Money

1907), the Banque de France was always prepared to give assistance; Britain relied also on the reserves of India. By 1913 the French central bank could almost be described as playing the role of a type of European (and indeed international) 'lender of last resort'.

Neither the First World War nor the ensuing economic and political upheavals destroyed this co-operation between some central banks, and in 1936 the Banque de France, the Federal Reserve Fund and the Bank of England made arrangements for mutual assistance which have continued until the present time. What was destroyed however was European and International stability, and much of Europe's economic strength was diminished. The Second World War simply destroyed what remained of Europe's economic strength.

This collapse of the European and the world economic and monetary system had three very important positive results, both theoretical and practical. At the international level, thinking and discussions about a future world monetary and trade system took place between the Allies throughout the latter years of the war and two major plans (the Keynes and White Plans) for a new world monetary order were produced. The subsequent adoption of the White Plan meant that the two main aims of international monetary policy were to be fixed exchange rates and convertibility, and gold was reconfirmed in its position of pre-eminence.

At a national level, important rethinking about future national economic policy took place in France, Germany (West), the Netherlands and the United

The Theory of Integration and Western Europe 25

Kingdom. The economic philosophy of the first two countries was to have an important influence on the evolution of the European Economic Community.

Finally, the catastrophe of the Second World War meant that there was a great resurgence of the European movement and of interest in economic integration in general. It was felt that because Europe had not been united in the inter-war years much economic progress had been lost, and so the best future for Western Europe lay in greater economic co-operation – as well as in political unity.

Before examining the main contributions made to the theory of economic integration and their relevance to 'Europe and money', it would be wise to examine the main tenets of the economic philosophy of West Germany and France, because without an awareness of the influence of these philosophies on the Treaty of Rome and on the European Economic Community it becomes difficult to fit the Common Market into the theoretical framework of economic integration.

The work of the German Social Market Economy School of economic philosophy is really most important. The main exponent of this philosophy at the moment – and one who had a great influence on the writing of the Treaty of Rome – is Mueller-Armack, who belongs to the tradition of Eucken, Schneider and the Freiburg School. Fundamentally the members of this school support a well-functioning market system because it could 'satisfy the multifarious individuals' demands effectively, and the economists made the value judgements that it was the individuals who mattered'.[1] The main difference between the old extreme neo-liberals and the supporters of the Social Market School is that the latter believe that it is the responsibility of the state to create and protect the framework in which the economy is to work. They believe, for example, that there is a need for an anti-monopoly policy, and that competition rules must be established and consumers protected at the same time. This implies, at a social level, that consumers are 'members of social, economic and political groups whose interests need to be represented and reconciled'. This emphasis on small groupings is an important cornerstone of the philosophy of this school of economic thought.

The main influence which the Social Market School has had on the Treaty of Rome and the subsequent evolution of the Community has been the great emphasis on competition and the control of concentration. This consideration is in conflict with the economic thinking which existed in France in the late 1940s and the 1950s, which preferred state planning and a uniformity of social charges and benefits (for example, the principle of equal pay, as embodied in the Treaty of Rome). The main exponents of this thinking were Monnet, Uri and Philip. Their support for state planning, in the early phases, also included a desire for state ownership of key sectors of the economy, while they expected the state at all times to influence national capital investment through its purchasing policy. It was French insistence which led to the creation of a medium-term plan in the Community.

Before examining the main contributions to the

The Theory of Integration and Western Europe 27

theory of economic integration we have seen two conflicting philosophical schools of economic thought at the outset of the infant Common Market. On the one hand we have the German (West) Social Market Economy School with its emphasis on competition. On the other, we have the French School of Planning with its additional support for uniformity of social charges and benefits. These conflicting influences have been one of the reasons for some of the lack of agreement in the Community.

Until now we have looked at two groups of economic philosophers who were intimately concerned with the rebuilding of their countries after the Second World War. In both cases, the fundamental aim of reconstruction was successfully achieved, and it was therefore normal that both schools of thought should wish to attempt to impose their model on the European Economic Community. In both cases the banking system had helped with the reconstruction of West Germany and France. In the former case it was a result of the closer links between the banks and industry; in the latter, it was largely because of strong government control of the banking and money systems. However neither school of thought had directed its attention very much to the question of trade, although the Social Market School did see trade as a desirable source of competition. The trade issue in a customs union (as distinct from a free trade area) had been examined by Viner[2] in his pioneering book, *The Customs Union Issue*, in 1950. Viner had already been concerned with this issue and the study of European economic problems in the 1920s and the 1930s, but this was his major work. Until this book appeared, the majority of economists had assumed that most moves towards free trade were good. Viner, however, pointed out that customs unions did not necessarily constitute a move in this direction because there were always two possible effects from such unions. These effects were:

trade creation
and/or
trade diversion.

In the former case if there was a move from a high-cost to a low-cost producer (as a result of the union) there was trade creation of a positive nature. If, as in the latter case, production was diverted from low-cost to high-cost producers then the result was negative. These considerations have proved to be rather important in the case of the Common Market.

In the economic sense Viner was concerned with production effects; he assumed the classical theory of constant costs with unchanged consumption patterns; and he expected a greater possibility of trade creation through competition – the greater the similarity among the different economies in the customs union the greater the degree of overlapping. Thus he was considering inter-country substitution.

Viner also examined a number of rather important considerations which were not exclusively economic in character. He suggested the possibility of making administrative economies through the creation of a central administration which would replace the individual national ones. He looked back at the teach-

The Theory of Integration and Western Europe

ings of the German Historical School which recommended (particularly in Europe) the union of groups of countries to enable them to increase their strength when negotiating at an international level (especially *vis-à-vis* the United States). Lastly he suggested the possibility of countries giving up immediate economic advantages when joining a customs union in exchange for more long-term economic and political advantages.

Although at the strictly economic level Viner was concerned almost exclusively with trade, his trade creation effect is in reality a form of welfare effect. Meade[3] was very much concerned with trade welfare considerations and examined this question from two different angles. He studied the measurement of the real welfare aspects of increases in imports in the volume of some goods compared with decreases in others. He was also concerned with the social welfare costs (for which some form of substitution would have to be found in a customs union) incurred through the decrease in government revenue occasioned by the removal of tariffs.

Meade's first consideration falls very much in the same category as that of Gehrels and Lipsey and Lancaster, who were concerned with inter-commodity substitution. They believed this to be a gap in the reasoning of Viner, though Spraos did not agree with them on this point.

Lipsey and Lancaster[4] considered that a customs union implied a move from an optimum state to an indeterminate state. They believed that it was difficult to satisfy all the optimum conditions for Paretian welfare optimisation and therefore came up with the idea of 'the theory of second best'. In their famous article they more specifically stated: 'if it is impossible to satisfy all the optimum conditions (in this case to make all relative prices equal to all rates of transformation in production), then a change which brings about the satisfaction of some of the optimum conditions (in this case making some relative prices equal to some rates of transformation in production) may make things better or worse.'

Both Meade and Lipsey considered that a net increase in the volume of trade – whether occasioned by a move from a low to a high cost source of production or the reverse – implied a net increase in economic welfare. Furthermore, Lipsey, writing in 1960, assumed that the tariff revenue collected by a government would be either returned to the consumers in the form of subsidies or spent by the government.

Developing the welfare argument somewhat further, Johnson,[5] very probably with his eye on the Treaty of Rome and the Common Market agricultural policy, considered that welfare benefits might accrue through income transfers made with the proceeds from tariff revenues. In fact, governments might decide to favour some sector(s) of the economy. Johnson considered that such a policy might be admissible in the case of a country which wished to industrialise its economy.

The works of all the economists which have been hitherto examined have tended to lead us away both from dynamic considerations in general and from 'Europe and money' in particular. At this point it is

The Theory of Integration and Western Europe

interesting to return to the European Economic Community. Two writers wrote specifically about the trade, dynamic and welfare possibilities of the E.E.C., and both went so far as to consider the creation of an economic and monetary union. These economists were Scitovsky[6] and Balassa;[7] their work has a particular relevance to our banking and monetary considerations.

Like Viner, Meade, Tinbergen and Balassa, Scitovsky favoured a large customs union area because such an area would tend to be more conducive to the utilisation of economies of scale and the principles of standardisation and specialisation. Also, through competition, he anticipated an efficient relocation of productive resources. He emphasised correctly the important dynamic role of capital investment but perhaps slightly less correctly the necessity of creating a European capital market. He warned, nevertheless, that the danger existed that capital would tend to move to the richer nations. He therefore believed that an integrated employment policy should take precedence over an integrated capital market. In this connection the public allocation of funds should be carefully planned and channelled through a supranational public works authority, endowed with fiscal and monetary powers. Scitovsky strongly stressed the need for supranationality in the Common Market.

He examined the evolution of an economic and monetary union, and thought it wise to examine the role of the Federal Reserve Board in the United States since this might serve as a model for a future European central banking system. Similarly the example of London should be examined as a possible model for a European Capital Market. Although Scitovsky desired stability, he did nevertheless recommend a policy of flexible exchange rates.

Returning to the dynamic considerations, he thought that the Common Market would be an attractive proposition to American capital but uttered a word of caution about the possibilities of specialisation and concentration. He also warned of the dangerous possibility of European monopolies replacing national ones. However, he correctly believed that there existed only a small possibility of a heavy relocation of manufacturing output among different European countries. Rather, he believed that the relocation would take place within countries. In this sense he has been proved correct, since during the period 1961–9 there were 1861 national mergers and 257 inter-country mergers in the European Economic Community.

The next major contribution to the more dynamic aspects of economic integration theory was made by Balassa. He placed great emphasis on the dynamic effects of economies of scale (an aspect of the division of labour) and in so doing placed himself in the same school of thought as Byé (1950) and Ohlin (1956), both of whom believed that increasing returns were associated with an enlarged market. Balassa believed that factor mobility was necessary for efficient resource allocation – although he did consider that some European policy co-ordination would be necessary – though not to the same supranational degree as

The Theory of Integration and Western Europe

that proposed by Byé, Philip and Scitovsky. Here also, in direct opposition to Philip, he believed that any harmonisation of social systems (social security charges and benefits) would be positively harmful.

Balassa examined the question of fiscal harmonisation as well as the creation of an economic and monetary union. He looked at the advantages and disadvantages of using an origin or destination principle when applying a value added tax. In this respect, he considered it wise to examine all taxes when embarking upon a programme of fiscal harmonisation.

When looking at the creation of an economic and monetary union he was less optimistic than Scitovsky was when considering the Federal Reserve Board as a possible model for the E.E.C. Indeed, he wondered whether the use of treasury paper would iron out regional disparities. He bore in mind also the important question of the equilibrium of the union *vis-à-vis* third parties.

In his work, Balassa went to great lengths to emphasise the dynamic effects of economies of scale and specialisation in a customs union. He correctly believed that these effects (especially when based on the encouragement given to increased capital investment) would lessen the possible negative economic and trade effects on third parties. Finally, a timely word of warning: Balassa wondered whether there would not be a once and for all increase in trade among the members of a customs union and therefore whether it might not prove necessary to constantly enlarge the union.

Hitherto economists have put forward the following

basic reasons for economic integration. They see, in the dynamic sense, the possibility of the use of economies of scale, specialisation of production and an improvement in efficiency through competition. Further, they foresee changes in terms of trade for the union *vis-à-vis* the rest of the world and changes (improvements) in the rate of economic growth. They assume, however, the existence of the following conditions: free competition in commodity and factor movements; zero transport costs; the mobility of other factors in the union which were formerly immobile; fixed exchange rates, unless otherwise stated; the existence of only one economic barrier – tariffs; and the absence of all domestic economic and trade distortions.

When the European Economic Community had been in existence for a number of years, several economists began to re-examine the theory of customs unions. Thus, in 1965, in an article which contained an innovatory[8] model, Cooper and Massell asked the basic question as to why nations entered into customs unions. They were not satisfied that this particular arrangement was the optimal one and even went so far as to ask why nations did not practise a non-discriminatory tariff.

Nevertheless these two economists, in examining customs unions more closely, maintained that the outcome depended on what happened both to income and industrial output. They also believed that the potential gains from a customs union would be larger if the countries concerned had a steeply rising marginal cost of production, if there existed a social preference for industrial production, if the countries' economies were complementary, and, if no country dominated the others in industrial production. Having said all this, they accused the countries of the Common Market of indulging in 'market swapping'.

Reference has already been made to the observations of Johnson in 1965, with particular reference to the E.E.C., who suggested that there might exist within certain communities a 'collective or public preference for certain types of economic activity'. Thus nations might decide to subsidise sectors directly through taxation, to make indirect subsidies through tax concessions, or to protect sectors through tariffs. The last-mentioned method is normally most palatable to the domestic public.

The last major contribution to the theory of economic integration was that made by Krauss[9] in 1972, when, having examined the works of many economists, he reached the conclusion that the creation of the European Economic Community was indeed a political decision.

At this point the fundamental question which must be asked is whether in trade, growth, concentration, specialisation, money and banking the European Economic Community has or has not fulfilled any of the theories and forecasts which we have examined. Has the Community become the great market free of obstacles to factor movements? Has the Community been an example of trade creation and/or diversion? And has the right of establishment become a fact of life in the E.E.C.?

Beginning with the Viner thesis we can note, in the

first twelve years of the Community's existence, trade creation with evidence of diversion mainly in the agricultural sector. During the same period, there has been evidence of the role played by the dynamic factors as suggested by Balassa and Scitovsky.(A number of economists, especially de la Vinelle, Tinbergen and Verdoorn, have arrived at varying quantitative conclusions as to the precise role of the removal of tariffs in this connection.) Capital investment and growth of income have been satisfactorily high – probably triggered off by the workings of the theory of expectations on the part of governments and business men. It is probably this factor which has been responsible for the growth in trade, not only within the Community, but also between the Common Market and third parties.

The Vinerian thesis was further demonstrated during the Kennedy Round negotiations when the Community negotiated as one body *vis-à-vis* the United States. One might discern something of another Vinerian thesis in Britain's membership of the E.E.C. Here, Britain appears to have been willing to forego immediate economic benefits in exchange for long-term economic and political considerations.

An area of constant controversy – and apparent achievement – in the Common Market has been the common agricultural policy. In this case a definite preference for this sector of the economy is obvious and income transfers have been made. This situation tends to give support to the Johnson thesis.

By 1968 the Community had apparently achieved the free movement of capital and labour, though the majority of migrants did come from without the Community. These facts would tend to indicate that the competition – to which so many economists have given their support – was in the process of materialising. Indeed, one can say that the field of competition and the control of concentration has been one of the most active achievements to the credit of the E.E.C., and the area where the influence of Mueller-Armack has been all-pervading. And yet this area is most paradoxical, as although Mueller-Armack, Viner, Balassa, Scitovsky and others all desire competition, some of the economists also desire specialisation – which implies concentration. This is indeed a dilemma, because while the Commission's lawyers actively encourage competition, the Community does desire to create enterprises of international dimensions. The situation is further complicated by the non-existence (at the time of writing) of a European Company Law and a European Banking Law. This unacceptable situation probably partly explains the absence of a greater number of inter-state mergers and implantation of companies and banks within the different countries of the Common Market. True, international banking syndicates had evolved in the 1960s and at the beginning of the present decade,[10] but this development tends to emphasise a monopolistic situation and to give some weight to the accusation of 'market swapping' (or sharing) made by Cooper and Massell. In the particular case of Italy, as will be examined in a future book on banking, the absence of a Community banking law not only prevents a European penetration in the Italian market, but also prevents inter-regional penetration within Italy itself!

Thus, in the Community, we have faced a paradoxical situation. On the one hand articles 85 and 86 of the Treaty of Rome go some way in encouraging competition. On the other, the absence of European Banking and Company Laws (among other reasons) have tended to limit inter-country penetration and instead to have encouraged mergers within the member states themselves.

In the case of the use of articles 85 and 86, the Commission has been most active. Until 1970 there was an almost exclusive concern with the former article (dealing with horizontal and vertical agreements). In this the criterion used has been the situation in which a company obtains a 'distinct economic advantage'. In such situations obligatory notification is the rule and complaints may be made by third parties. The result was that by 1971 some 37,000 notifications had been made – of which about 30,000 concerned exclusive dealing; it was alleged that such agreements gave 'absolute territorial protection' to the companies concerned. Among this latter group six were banned outright. From 1971 onwards use has been made by the Commission of article 86 in order to contol mergers. Here two criteria have been used: the basic criterion of the 'dominant firm' (with a control of between 50 and 55 per cent of the market) and a 'restriction of the choice of the consumers'. Finally, in 1973, legislation was proposed (together with a draft European Company Law) to deal with mergers, since it was felt that some mergers would be necessary if the Common Market were to survive in the international market. These drafts are still being discussed by the Council of Ministers.

In reality, as Jacquemin[11] has shown in a recent article, there has been a great concentration in particular areas within individual countries. Thus there has been great concentration in oil, chemicals, steel, electrical engineering and automobiles. Further, as the following statistics indicate, the top E.E.C. firms have gradually increased their share of the market. Also (though not shown in this table) there has been a greater concentration in Belgium, the Netherlands and West Germany than in France and Italy.

Top E.E.C. firms : share of G.N.P. (the 'Six')

	1960 %*	1965 %	1970 %
Top 4	5·8	6·8	8·1
Top 20	20·9	22·5	29·0
Top 50	35·0	35·0	45·7

* As a percentage of 100%

Our examination leads us to make the following conclusions. At the trade level, trade creation has tended to outweigh trade diversion. There has been (one assumes, due to dynamic factors) a great growth in inter-Community trade and in trade between the E.E.C. and third parties. A qualified and selective mobility of capital and labour has been achieved. In the field of banking and business, the absence of European legislation has made it easier for multi-nationals (especially American companies) to implant themselves in the Common Market rather than to encourage inter-state mergers in the Community. The absence of such legislation – together with other economic factors – has probably led to the evolution of the Euro-dollar market rather than the creation of a purely European capital market. Nevertheless, despite these facts and the active use by the Commission of articles 85 and 86 of the Treaty of Rome, a great concentration among banks and companies has developed within the member states of the European Economic Community. Thus one can conclude that the theories of the works of the different economists have partially materialised. Finally one can observe, in two important areas, an increase in the welfare of the inhabitants of the Common Market: their wealth has increased and their choice of goods has widened. However their choice would have been even greater had a greater inter-state penetration by companies – but especially by banks – been possible. During the coming years, apart from any moves towards economic and monetary union, a definite move towards inter-penetration would do much to increase the welfare of the inhabitants of the European Economic Community.

3 Optimum Currency Area: Theories Re-examined

Before undertaking this re-examination, two major considerations should be borne in mind. First, an optimum currency area is a different animal from an economic and monetary union. An optimum currency area comprises a group of countries whose currencies are linked together through fixed exchange rates. Optimum currency areas have consisted of countries at quite different stages of economic development. An economic and monetary union implies not only fixed exchange rates, but also common economic, fiscal and monetary policies as well as a common currency. It is because of these facts that it is so difficult to achieve an economic and monetary union on a strict voluntary basis.

The second consideration which we have to bear in mind is that the major contributions to the subject of optimum currency areas have been made at different times – when international monetary conditions differed quite considerably. Thus, when the two pioneering contributions were being made (in 1961 and

1963), the pound sterling, and to some degree the dollar, were experiencing difficulties – but fixed exchange rates and convertibility were the order of the day. However, when the second group of contributions was being made (in the early 1970s), 'floating' was becoming increasingly accepted and economic and regional differences within the European Economic Community were becoming more obvious.

THE MAJOR CONTRIBUTIONS

The major contributions to the study of optimum currency areas have been made by Mundell (1961), McKinnon (1963), Kenen (1969), Fleming (1971), Onida (1972), Magnifico and Corden (1973), Presley and Dennis (1976).

Mundell, in his original contribution,[1] stresses the difference between a currency area with a single currency and one with several currencies. The basic difference here is between interregional and international adjustments. At the international level the basic question becomes one of whether surplus countries will themselves accept inflation internally or whether the deficit countries will be forced to deflate. In contrast, 'in a currency area comprising many regions and a single currency, the pace of inflation is set by the willingness of central authorities to allow unemployment in deficit regions'.

To Mundell, the fundamental problem is the fact that 'a currency area of either type cannot prevent both unemployment and inflation among its members'. He defines optimality in terms of ability to

Optimum Currency Area: Theories Re-examined 43

stabilise national employment and price levels, and stresses that the existence of more than one currency area in the world implies variable exchange rates. Logically then, according to Mundell, the optimum currency area in this case is the region.

This emphasis on the region as being the optimum currency area is really most important, because although flexible exchange rates are the equilibrating mechanism between the different optimum currency areas, it is factor mobility which is the equilibrating mechanism within the areas. In fact to Mundell an optimum currency area is precisely a region in which there exists factor mobility. It is this part of the theory which has been most criticised by economists. The author believes that Mundell might have had different historical examples in mind when he was constructing his theory.[2] Thus it is feasible that Mundell might have been thinking of the example of the British Empire and Dominions or Britain and the United States in the nineteenth and the early part of the present century. In these cases there existed free factor mobility which tended to move towards the New World to develop agriculture and industry. It is also possible that Mundell had in mind a complete economic and monetary union *tout court*. Whichever of these examples were in his mind, it is precisely this emphasis on factor mobility which has enraged some economists. The reason for this lies in the difference in the experience of the nineteenth century and the 1960s. In the former, capital and labour tended to move to areas where agriculture and industry needed developing, whereas in the 1960s capital and labour tended to move to already highly developed and wealthy centres. Thus this latter development highlighted the regional problem and the difficulties involved in making a complete economic and monetary union acceptable without first solving the regional problem. Nevertheless if Mundell is taking an optimum currency area and an economic and monetary union as being one and the same thing, then certainly one of the pre-conditions of a complete union is free factor mobility.

The next contribution to the study of optimum currency area theory was made by McKinnon[3] two years later. McKinnon places great emphasis on the necessity of first analysing the degree of 'openness' of the economy and the ratio of 'tradable' to 'non-tradable' goods. In whichever category a country finds itself, McKinnon emphasises the importance of internal price stability and full employment. According to the degree of 'openness' of an economy, the use of different weapons in demand management are recommended. Thus, in the case of an open ecenomy working close to full employment, internal fiscal and monetary controls are recommended; in a less open economy, exchange-rate variations are suggested to correct balance of payment disequilibria.

McKinnon also turns his attention to the question of the currencies of relatively small countries. Here the problem arises of the liquidity value or 'moneyness' of such currencies. These countries are advised either to peg their currencies together or to peg them to those of their major trading partner. In the latter case a number of examples immediately spring to mind: Britain and Eire, the Netherlands and West Germany, Belgium and Luxemburg.

McKinnon does not implicitly reject Mundell's thesis of factor mobility but tends to recommend this – when all else fails. Further, unlike Mundell, he distinguishes between geographical and industrial mobility.

The next major contribution was that made by Kenen in 1969.[4] He believes that the criterion which should be used to define an optimum currency area is 'complementarity'. However, he does align himself somewhat with Mundell's thesis since he uses free labour mobility as the equilibrating factor. Thus he considers that 'exchange rates should be fixed between single-product regions when labour moves freely between them'. In contrast with Mundell, however, Kenen's equilibrating mechanism seems to be of a longer and more structural nature: one could imagine the example of agricultural and industrial products. In such a hypothetical situation, a decline in the demand for agricultural products and an increase in the demand for industrial products would lead to a movement of labour from the agricultural product region to the industrial product region.

The contributions made by Onida and Magnifico[5] – and then by Corden[6] – belong to the busy period of plans for and studies about economic and monetary union in the European Economic Community. They are therefore more naturally concerned with the possibility of fixing exchange rates between the member states of the Community and the eventual creation of a common currency. Onida and Magnifico are particularly aware of the regional problem, and of the danger of a premature introduction of fixed exchange rates without first solving this problem. They are consequently somewhat critical of Mundell's use of the free mobility of factors of production as the equilibrating mechanism in an economic and monetary union. Here it should be noted that both economists appear to confuse an optimum currency area with an economic and monetary union.

Onida's dissatisfaction with Mundell's equilibrating mechanism leads him to set down an action programme of economic development for the European Economic Community – without actually defining a criterion for either an optimum currency area or an economic and monetary union. However, Onida's emphasis on economic and regional development lead us to believe that in reality. Onida might in both cases use a similar level of economic and regional development as his criterion. Until the time for fixed exchange rates is ripe, he favours parity changes, capital controls and inter-government co-operation.

Magnifico is rather sophisticated in his definition of a criterion for an optimum currency area. The common factor to him is 'a similar propensity to inflate'. Unless this quality is common to all the member states of such an area, speculation will take place and it will be difficult if not impossible to maintain fixed exchange rates. In the specific case of the Common Market Magnifico is concerned, like Onida, with finding ways of bringing the member states up to the same level of economic and regional development. In this way, one can assume that a 'similar propensity to inflate' will also be achieved.

Corden is concerned with monetary integration and therefore distinguishes between a pseudo-union (really, the intermediate period) and a full monetary union which implies fixed exchange rates, convertibility and capital market integration.

Corden is somewhat critical of McKinnon's views about the likelihood of money illusion on the part of the workers in an open economy. Nevertheless he does go some way with McKinnon when he considers the case of a fully integrated customs union and a very small open economy. In the former case, he says, 'if an economy is very open – like a French department or Scotland – one might just as well fix its exchange rate in relation to its main trading partners'. In the latter case, the country would not be a 'feasible' currency area since its inhabitants would tend to prefer foreign currency to their own money. In this case the country should link its currency with that of its main trading partner.

Corden gives some support to the thesis of Mundell regarding factor mobility. He points out that 'mobility of labor makes it less necessary to adjust real wages upward or downward in response to changing demand and supply conditions, and hence less necessary to use exchange-rate alterations as an instrument of real-wage adjustment. It follows that the more mobile labor is within the union, the less the costs of an exchange-rate union.' But having said this Corden still considers that 'labor mobility is an inadequate substitute for exchange-rate flexibility, though it certainly reduces the costs, possibly substantially so, of exchange-rate inflexibility, and even yields gains of its own.'

On this latter point, however, the author would utter a word of caution. A semi-permanent state of exchange-rate variations (under 'floating', for example) may make the wage differentials so different between countries that workers in the countries whose currencies are constantly being devalued may choose to migrate! This is indeed a paradoxical situation. On the other hand Corden, in his criticism of McKinnon, takes the example of West Germany (a surplus country) which has attempted to isolate itself from imported inflation through successive revaluations of the deutschmark. Nevertheless West Germany's small but important (and very open) trading partner, the Netherlands, has kept its currency closely linked with the German one.

Lastly, Corden does agree with McKinnon concerning the desirability of stability. Here he points out that if problems are internal and structural in nature, internal financial and/or monetary instruments should be used for demand management. If, however, the problems are macro-economic and external in nature, exchange-rate variations should be used.

Fleming[7], looking more specifically at the European Economic Community and its decision to embark upon an economic and monetary union, is concerned about the possibility of certain developments taking place. He believes it possible that deficit countries may be forced to accept high levels of unemployment.

Optimum Currency Area: Theories Re-examined 49

Unlike Mundell he does not see labour mobility as a panacea, because labour mobility within the Common Market tends to be low compared with that in the United States. He is also dubious about the equilibrating role of capital, pointing out that in the medium term, where a state of instability exists, capital mobility may be a disequilibrating agent. He suggests that even if high cost centres use interest rates to attract capital, they may not be completely successful in their attempts. The author would point out that in recent years changes in interest rates have been relatively ineffective and, as he forewarned in 1969, capital tends to continue to flow into the highly developed areas of Western Europe.

Some of the problems we have been examining could possibly be removed through the equalisation of factor costs. The problem here is, how is this to be achieved? Haberler,[8] did, some time ago, set down such a list of preconditions which would have to be fulfilled if factor costs were to be made equal; unfortunately these preconditions are so complex that it is difficult to see how they could be attained.

Presley and Dennis[9] have tried more recently to relate the various optimum currency area theories to the real world. They brush aside the use of the expression 'optimality' as far as the European Economic Community is concerned, but nevertheless believe that the Community is a strong candidate for economic and monetary union. When examining the contributions made by different economists to optimum currency area theories, they consider that Mundell's contribution is not applicable to the Common Market because of its inherent labour immobility. In contrast, due to the Community's ever-increasing 'openness' and diversity of production, it would seem largely to satisfy the criteria of McKinnon and Kenen. Lastly, they consider that a trade-off between unemployment and inflation does not exist in the long run. To them this fact is the main argument in favour of an economic and monetary union. Where the natural levels of unemployment have been reached, exchange rates should be linked between the currencies of the member states.

This final proposal regarding the 'natural' level of unemployment is unlikely to go unchallenged by economists since it is extremely difficult to define the 'natural' level for a country. The difficulties are increased still further by the changes which occur over time in the economic structure of a country. A way out of the dilemma would be to use Magnifico's criterion for linking exchange rates together: 'a similar propensity to inflate'.

THE AUTHOR'S CONSIDERATIONS

A certain confusion appears to exist about optimum currency areas and economic and monetary unions, which are not the same animals. There does nevertheless exist one element which is common to both – fixed exchange rates. In the case of an optimum currency area composed of different national currencies, however, adjustment is essentially international and the use of specific instruments depends both on the degree of 'openness' of the economy concerned and on the possible reactions of that country's trading partners.

In the case of an economic and monetary union, that is an area which has one currency and common and centralised economic policy instruments, the problem is essentially regional, and the central authorities – particularly if the union is not an 'open' one – have greater freedom in their use of instruments for restoring equilibrium than in the former case.

At this point we shall examine first the specific case of the European Economic Community and second the international monetary situation. In both cases reference will be made to the applicability of the works hitherto examined, and some proposals will be made in an attempt to solve current problems and to push the E.E.C. more realistically towards the achievement of an economic and monetary union.

At the present time one can observe a form of *de facto* economic and monetary union in the Common Market (West Germany, the Benelux countries and Denmark) while the other members belong to a zone of managed floating. The question which must be asked is, do the Five display any common qualities which allow us to explain the linking together of their currencies? The common factor which one can immediately observe is the high degree of 'openness' and interdependence of these economies. An important part of their gross national product is traded, and the majority of this trade is carried out among themselves. Furthermore, two small countries link their currencies closely with their major trading partners: the Netherlands link the guilder with the deutschmark and the Luxemburg franc is linked with the Belgian one.

Other common features are also visible. With the exception of Denmark these countries display a fairly similar degree of inflation and they are also at a similar high level of economic development. Likewise, although a great concentration of population exists in the western part of the Netherlands and in Belgium, and West Germany has frontier regions which are less prosperous than the central ones, none of the Five display the great regional disparities which are to be found among the Four. Lastly – a factor which is sometimes ignored by economists – these five countries are in close geographical proximity to each other.

The factors just enumerated lead us to examine the types of adjustment instruments used both within the Five and between them and the outside world. In general they prefer to use fiscal and monetary instruments for demand management. This preference would seem to give support to the McKinnon thesis. It has not, however, excluded revaluations of the deutschmark and – consequently – of the Dutch guilder.

The situation concerning factor movements is less clear. Both West Germany and the Netherlands try to discourage inflows of capital. Free movement of labour officially exists, and West Germany has benefited enormously from a heavy inflow of migrants over the past two decades. Here again, however, the situation is nebulous because most of the migrants come from countries which are outside the E.E.C., while the Five (especially the Netherlands and West Ger-

Optimum Currency Area: Theories Re-examined

many) maintain a careful control over migrant inflows through residence and health restrictions. On the other hand in all countries of the European Economic Community there have been major movements of labour between different sectors of the economy.

Finally, it is necessary with regard to the Five to consider the possible existence of complementarity and/or comparative advantages. These countries are all heavily industrialised and only the Netherlands and Denmark can be considered to have an important agricultural sector. If, however, size is an important comparative advantage, then this is West Germany. On the other hand, in such a union, the prosperity of a small state like Luxemburg would seem to be paradoxical, although it may be explained by Luxemburg's enjoyment of important fiscal privileges (allowed by the E.E.C.) which constitute a comparative advantage.

This examination does underline the existence of two groups of countries within the Common Market which are at two different stages of economic development. This division is further accentuated by the periodic (now, almost perpetual) speculation which is fuelled by the huge and volatile masses of 'hot money' with which the world has to live. This is an important development which forces us to take a completely new look at international monetary problems. However, let us remain for the moment within the Common Market.

As has already been seen, we have two different groups of countries in the Community, with one group (the Five) already forming a *de facto* economic and monetary union. The similar qualities exhibited by these countries have led some people to propose a more accelerated development of their union. If such a plan were adopted, what policies should the Four follow? In the first place, there are considerable differences between these countries. Italy and France for example conduct a major amount of their trade within the European Economic Community and a reasonable amount with each other; we could at least expect in the future a linking of their currencies together and, in the long term, a linking of their currencies with those of the Five, thus forming a large optimum currency area.

The case of both the United Kingdom and the Republic of Ireland is rather different. Compared with the economies of the other member states of the E.E.C. the British economy is not a particularly 'open' one, nor does Britain conduct a lot of her trade with the Community. It is for these reasons that the author and J. R. Presley have always recommended that the United Kingdom use parity changes when facing balance-of-payments problems – and particularly during an intermediate phase of economic and monetary union. Indeed as long as the British economy remains relatively closed it is difficult to see why Britain should join an economic and monetary union, unless the Community were prepared to allow Britain similar or greater fiscal and/or other privileges than those granted to Luxemburg. The British situation is further complicated by the overseas sterling balances held in London and the large volatile masses of 'hot' money which are currently moving about the world. A pre-

Optimum Currency Area: Theories Re-examined

condition of any move towards the creation of closer links between the Community and Britain in the monetary field would be the funding of sterling balances.

The case of Ireland is different. Ireland has for decades conducted most of its trade with the United Kingdom. Thus even when political independence was gained the Republic continued to link the Irish currency with the pound sterling. There was, nevertheless, a nuance in this link. Both before and since independence there has been massive migration from the Republic to the United Kingdom. It is precisely this situation which troubles both Onida and Magnifico because they fear that a premature linking together of currencies within the Community will lead to a massive movement of labour from the periphery to the centre.

However, in the case of Ireland, since her membership of the E.E.C. trade has increased with the Community and has tended to decrease with Britain. It is therefore likely that when Ireland conducts most of her trade with the rest of the Community, her currency will be linked with the currencies of her main trading partners.

Thus, among the Four, we have Britain on one side and France, Ireland and Italy on the other. Of the latter, France and Italy already conduct a major part of their trade within the Community but are undergoing structural changes which may be of a short- or medium-term nature. When these problems are solved, the currencies of these two countries will almost certainly be linked once again with those of their main Common Market trading partners. Similarly, although Ireland still conducts most of her trade with Britain, in the foreseeable future most of her trade will be conducted within the Community and the currency of this 'open' economy will most probably be linked with those of her main trading partners. In the meantime, as is already happening to a certain degree in the case of Italy, a transfer of resources from the Five to these countries could be envisaged, thus enabling them to rejoin the optimum currency area and *de facto* economic and monetary union more swiftly.

As already noted, the situation of the United Kingdom is rather different. The British economy is not a particularly 'open' one and the majority of trade is not conducted with the E.E.C. partners. Thus there appear to be few reasons why, for the time being, Britain should join either a Community optimum currency area or a *de facto* economic and monetary union. Should the rest of the Community desire Britain to join any of these monetary links, some arrangements for funding the overseas sterling balances would have to be made and some form of economic/monetary compensation be arranged. Here one could look back to the example of the unification of Germany, when Prussia gave to the city of Frankfurt am Main fiscal privileges which were more important than the economic strength of that city. This was done in order to mitigate possible negative effects which Frankfurt might have experienced after having joined the German union.

Any moves towards a European optimum currency

Optimum Currency Area: Theories Re-examined

area or an economic and monetary union, or any moves at a more international level towards fixed exchange rates, necessitate careful consideration of the problem of the masses of volatile 'hot' money which now exist. At this point we should turn towards this problem and the international monetary situation in general.

Ideally, under a system of floating exchange rates, one could envisage the position of two countries, A and B: suppose that country A has a surplus and country B a deficit, then we could imagine an appreciation of the currency of country A and a depreciation of that of country B. Other things being equal, the result of this development would be that eventually the goods of country A would, internationally, becme more expensive than those of country B and this would lead to an eventual balance of payments equilibrium. Equally, if free movement of labour exists, one might in the first instance imagine a movement of labour from country B to A, to take account of the high demand for country A's goods. Then as the goods of this country become more expensive and demand for the goods of country B increases, one could imagine a return of labour to the country of its origin – that is to country B. Again, a state of equilibrium would exist.

What, however, are some of the likely developments at the present time? First, the already mentioned masses of 'hot' money imply that any appreciation or depreciation of currencies might be more than is reasonably warranted by a balance of payments disequilibria. This, in turn, may imply further serious developments. Returning to the example of countries A and B, the currency of country A may appreciate so much that some of its goods may be priced out of the international market. In the case of country B, the prices of imports may rise so dramatically as to cause inflation and labour unrest. Some workers, particularly those among the liberal professions, may have a money illusion of wages in country A and may (though not unemployed) leave country B. In an extreme situation, the depreciation of the currency of country B may be so great that it will no longer be quoted on the foreign exchange markets. Also, attempts to use the interest rates to influence the flows of 'hot' money may lead to an interest-rate war.[10] All these possibilities imply that measures should be undertaken to sterilise some of the amounts of 'hot' money, and/or monetary discipline should be encouraged among nations which persistently maintain balance of payments deficits because of excessive consumption rather than because of a restructuring of industry and of their economy in general.

These considerations bring us back to our point of departure, optimum currency areas. Why are such areas necessary? They would seem to be necessary because they create zones of stability in a much troubled monetary world and because they link together major trading partners. Which criteria would imply the existence of an optimum currency area? According to the examination conducted in this study, we may list the following criteria: an 'open' economy linking its currency with its major trading partner(s), countries at a similar level of economic development

Optimum Currency Area: Theories Re-examined

with a 'similar propensity to inflate', and, probably, countries geographically reasonably close. What is the place of capital and labour mobility in such an area? This is both selective and complex, and is further complicated in north-western Europe by the generous social security benefits which may prove to be a disincentive to labour mobility. Thus, if one takes the example of the Five, there is capital mobility within the area – and in some cases between the area and third parties (note should be made of the successful existence of two money markets in the case of Belgium). There is, legally at least, labour mobility within the area, though this is carefully screened by the judicious issue of residence permits. However, there does also exist an important labour mobility between the Five and non-member states of the European Economic Community. This, like the internal mobility, tends to be sectoral and selective, and also tends to be sectorally intensified by the reluctance of nationals within the Five to work in certain areas of the economy, even when they are unemployed. Therefore to the criteria listed above we can add this further element – selective mobility of capital and labour both within the area and between it and third parties. Finally, the currencies of this optimum currency area do, for the time being, conduct a joint float against the dollar. If in the long run a system of 'stable but adjustable exchange rates' is the basis of the international monetary system, one can contemplate periodic adjustments between the currencies of different optimum currency areas and individual countries.

4 Towards a Monetary Union

Many volumes have been written about the economic and monetary union in the Common Market – so many that they may have tended to cloud the real issues. It is therefore perhaps useful to briefly recapitulate certain major facts at this point.

One of the most important facts – which should not be ignored – is that when in 1969 it was agreed to embark upon this union, the situation was indeed completely different from that existing today. There were many sound reasons why it was both feasible and necessary to move towards such a union. The original Six of the European Economic Community had achieved a surprising degree of economic integration – together with a relatively high mobility of the factors of production. They were and still are rather 'open' economies and the majority of their trade is carried out among themselves. Further, it was possible to say that, with the exception of the southern part of Italy, the Six had reached a somewhat similar degree of economic development. An additional technical factor which militated in favour of a linking together of exchange rates was the existence of the common agricultural policy and market which was best able to function in a system of relatively fixed exchange rates. Finally, although divergences between the French franc and the deutschmark had occurred in 1969, the world had not yet been confronted with the energy and monetary upheavals to which we have now become accustomed.

All the monetary plans were applicable to the Six, but new members of the European Economic Community were simply 'invited' to accept the Werner Report. This fact is really most important, because it implies that plans which had been designed for the countries which were so closely integrated would automatically fail if applied to countries where the economic and trading structure differed so much from that of the Six. Also, when the views of the two main schools of thought[1] – the 'economists' and the 'monetarists' – were being put forward, it seems that neither school really heeded the important qualities and defects of each other. Thus for example while the 'monetarists' did press for an early introduction of fixed exchange rates, they also stressed the necessity of almost simultaneously creating a well-endowed monetary fund which would help member states which might be confronted with balance of payments difficulties. The 'economists', on the other hand, while correctly assuming that it would be difficult to fix exchange rates between countries which were at a dissimilar stage of economic development, failed to make any proposals whatever concerning the means and policies which might be necessary in order to achieve this similarity.

These considerations, plus the international energy and monetary crises, have led to the splitting-up of the Community into two distinct economic groups, with the Five constituting an optimum currency area and a *de facto* economic and monetary union. This situation has led both ex-Chancellor Willy Brandt of West Germany and the Belgian Prime Minister, Léo Tindemans, to propose the creation of two different economic and monetary unions in the Common Market which would progress at different speeds. Although this suggestion has been greeted with undisguised hostility by many politicians, it seems to be a logical proposal because the Five are inevitably moving forwards together and constitute a zone of relative monetary stability. This proposal does not imply that the Community does not have economic and monetary achievements to its credit.[2] The Common Market has indeed achieved much, but some of the progress in the monetary field has been more symbolic than effective. Thus, a whole host of organisations and economic weapons exist, but they tend to be under-utilised.

The situation at the present time is one in which the Five are inevitably moving forwards together, without any policy as to how the Four will be brought back into the union. Before even making suggestions as to how these countries might be helped, the technical consideration which was made in the previous section regarding the United Kingdom should again be mentioned. Britain's economy is not very 'open' and the majority of her trade is not conducted with her partners in the European Economic Community. Thus it is difficult to see how Britain could join an economic and monetary union. Equally, it is difficult to see how the United Kingdom's exchange rates can be stabilised (even if there was a low level of inflation in Britain) until the overseas sterling balances are neutralised and means are found to sterilise some of the masses of 'hot' money which are currently in existence. The existence of this 'hot' money plus the inflationary potential of exchange-rate intervention also places limits on the ability of countries which possess strong currencies to intervene in the exchange markets to help weaker currencies. A final difficulty which will always impede the evolution of a successful economic and monetary union is the absence of a 'lender of last resort' and a lack of political will. Given all these considerations, if the European Economic Community believes that an economic and monetary union is both necessary and desirable, then the only policy worthy of consideration would seem to be one whereby such a union becomes so attractive that a member state which is technically eligible as a candidate for the union will ensure that it becomes and remains a member. One of the surer ways of achieving this aim would be through a greater reliance on fiscal harmonisation and the use of the Community Budget.

The important potenial of the budget has until recently tended to be obscured by the almost exclusive use of funds for the common agricultural policy. The situation has been further complicated by an insidious clinging by member states to the principle of *juste retour* and a certain lack of clarity about the basic principles, necessity and possible use of tax harmonisation. Nevertheless, since the Community has recently been in the process of acquiring its 'own' budget (a process started in 1971 and achieved by 1975), the Common Market now stands at a crossroads with regards to the future use of this important weapon. The use of the budget proper is also complemented by the Social Fund (with which the Commission may now take its own initiative) and the Regional Fund.

In 1975 the budget was made up of the following parts: the total revenue from member states from agricultural levies and duties on sugar *minus* administrative expenses; the total revenue from customs duties *minus* administrative expenses; and direct contributions from member states. New members do not yet fully conform to the first two requirements. The 1975 budget consisted of 5825 million units of account (equivalent to 0·7 per cent of the gross national product of the European Economic Community), of which over 80 per cent was used for agricultural price maintenance and structural reform.

Considerations about the Community budget must involve some examination of tax harmonisation, because future increases in funds will inevitably come from direct contributions which are based on a percentage of a generalised tax among all member states.*
Hitherto agreement on tax harmonisation has been concerned with two taxes, value-added tax and excise

* To be fully applicable in 1978.

duties, while corporation taxes are under examination and a report[8] on these taxes has been produced.

There are, apart from the necessity of financing the Community budget, very sound reasons why, in any moves towards a complete economic and monetary union, there must be tax harmonisation. These are the need to remove distortions to trade flows and factor movements, and the equal necessity of removing obstacles to internal capital flows and preventing third parties from gaining fiscal privileges in the customs union.

Any considerations about taxes must naturally take into account the principles of equality and efficiency in collection. Considerations on tax harmonisation, apart from taking into account these principles, must also heed national traditions. It is mainly for this reason that the Common Market decided to concentrate on the introduction of the value-added tax throughout the Community, although this tax does also act as a disincentive to *vertical integration*. In addition, it was felt that it would be easier to collect this type of tax in countries where evasion of personal income tax may be seen as a matter of personal honour as well as of self-enrichment!

A certain confusion has surrounded the principles associated with the value-added tax. Although the Commission, following the publication of the Neumark Report in 1962, considered that a *restricted origin* tax would be less likely to distort production flows, we do in fact have a tax based on a *selected destination* principle at the present time. Professor Prest has correctly pointed out that the Commission was wrong in its views about the principle of restricted origin, because this would indeed distort production location since there would be an encouragement given to entrepreneurs to invest in certain areas of the E.E.C. and not in others. On the other hand the destination principle influences sales and not the location of production.

Following the introduction of the value-added tax throughout the Community, a draft directive, published in 1973, proposed the harmonisation of the different rates by 1978.

As already mentioned, the other area where progress has been made is that concerning excise duties. Two of the main reasons why attention was drawn to these taxes were to remove obstacles to inter-Community trade and to prevent state monopolies. In 1970, the Community reached agreement on tobacco duties and the suppression of state monopolies in this field and also agreed to limit specific duties over the next four to five years.

Reference has already been made to the necessity of reaching some agreement on a general introduction of corporation tax and its harmonisation throughout the Community. The present varied situation in the Common Market does encourage third parties, who are working in some Common Market countries, to transfer funds and profits to countries outside the E.E.C. Such a situation naturally implies a loss of revenue to the Community. Further, a general corporation tax throughout the Common Market would also tend to discourage excessive amounts of retained profits (thus encouraging efficiency through the contact of companies with the money market) and would naturally encourage capital flows within the Community. An additional reason for the renewed interest in this tax is the possibility of using a certain percentage of the revenue from these taxes for financing the Community budget. Opinions are, however, somewhat divided about this matter.

At the present time the maximum possible levy, based on the value-added tax and used to finance the budget, is 1 per cent. It has been suggested that the increased needs of the Common Market may necessitate a levy of 4 per cent by 1980. In fact, in 1975 the levy used amounted to only 0·38 per cent! Thus, while Professor Dosser has suggested that since businesses will most likely reap the greatest advantages from the Common Market, then for reasons of social justice the Community should rely more on corporation tax for financing its budget, Professor Prest does not agree with this opinion. He points out that the value-added tax has already been introduced and, in fact, only a small percentage of the possible levy is used. Also in recent years wages and salaries have tended to increase more swiftly than profits, thus facilitating a transfer of wealth. The author would point out that, at a Community level, whether reliance is placed on one or both of the taxes, they will tend to act as a form of 'inbuilt stabiliser' because the actual revenue transferred to the budget by each member state will vary with the economic activity in each country.

Other suggestions about taxation have been more *avant-garde*. Concern has been expressed about regional problems, and some persons therefore go so far as to suggest the levying of special taxes on the wealthier and more concentrated areas of the Community; this revenue would then be transferred to the poorer areas. Other people have adopted a longer-term view whereby a real 'inbuilt stabiliser' would be created which would take the form of a centralisation of welfare taxes and benefits. Such a suggestion naturally belongs to the eventual more supranational situation which the Common Market may some day reach.

At this stage we should perhaps bear in mind that there exists no necessity of harmonising all taxes – providing they do not distort location of production and the flows of goods and capital within the Community, and provided they do not give fiscal privileges to third parties. Although it is not always wise to look to the United States as a model for the E.E.C., note should nevertheless be taken of the existence of a number of different state and local taxes in that country which do not impede production and trade flows.

If in the immediate future, the member states do not wish to increase their direct contributions to the budget, the use of the existing funds should be re-examined. One area where such a reappraisal is necessary is that concerned with agricultural policy. It is not really acceptable that so much finance is given to price maintenance. Should the Community wish to continue to support agriculture it should give greater emphasis to structural reform, and any further aid should come through the floating of Community loans or a direct access to the capital market by the countries concerned. In this way some element of accountability and control would enter the picture.

At a structural level, the suggestion made by Magnifico for the creation of a multi-role (development) bank and a dynamic use of the Social Fund (which may now initiate its own projects) deserve examination. The creation of such a bank and a more dynamic use of the Social Fund might, through structural projects, contribute towards bringing the Five and the Four closer together and might also succeed in making economic and monetary union a more attractive proposition to the member states of the European Economic Community.

There appears to exist very little disagreement among economists, to whichever school of thought they may belong, regarding the desire for structural changes among the economies of some of the nation states of the European Economic Community. Nor does there appear to be much opposition to the floating of loans, for specific purposes, by the Commission. As already mentioned the attractiveness of such loans lies in the quality of accountability which is automatically embodied in them. Further, these loans do use the specialised services of the different monetary centres of the Common Market and probably constitute the first steps on the road to the creation of a purely European capital market. Here one must admit that not a great deal has happened since the publication of the Segré Report in 1966. Nevertheless the author believes that the floating of Community loans is a means of creating both the European capital market and the economic and monetary union – by stealth – and through means which are attractive to all members.

The upheavals of the 1970s have tended to put in the shade some of the important proposals for the use of the unit of account and the Monetary Fund which have been made during the present decade; nor have the equally important proposals for the harmonisation of banking legislation received the attention which they deserve. We shall now examine the most significant of these proposals.

Four main groups of proposals have been made. The first of any magnitude were made by Magnifico and Williamson, in 1972; by Mundell, in 1973; by the Commission, in the same year; and by a group of economists who published their proposals in *The Economist*, in November 1975. Giersch, Meade and Neubauer have also made comments about the basic principles in a later study, published by the E.E.C. Commission in 1973.

At the outset one can say that nearly all economists have agreed about the creation of a unit of account which should be composed of a basket or *panier* of the currencies of the different member states. Such a unit does now exist, as does also the European Monetary Fund. Many economists also believed that this unit of account should be used as an intervention currency since so much of the trade of the Community is internal.

Magnifico and Williamson[4] wished to see the European Monetary Fund transformed into a kind of European Central Bank, which would in fact launch the unit of account – the 'Europa'. Consequently, the national banks would have the responsibility of intervening to defend the rate between their national currencies and the Europa. In turn, the European Central Bank would defend the Europa against the dollar rate.

When the member states had paid into this bank a specified proportion of their reserves plus a quota of their national currency, they would eventually receive in exchange deposits denominated in Europas, and the bank would make open-market operations like a central bank. The bank would then control overall monetary policy and would encourage the growth of the Europa as a private monetary asset, mainly by acting as a central bank to the commercial banks in the Europa market.

Since these proposals were and still are somewhat supranational in character both economists made a number of suggestions, which, if adopted, they hoped would make the Europa more acceptable. Thus they proposed that issues/loans floated by the European Investment Bank should be quoted in Europas. Similarly, parts of national debts could be financed in these units and commercial banks could hold some reserves in Europas. Taxes could be paid in these units, and the European Central Bank could eventually offer clearing-house facilities as the 'lender of last resort'.

Mundell, in his contribution to the study published by the Commission in 1973,[5] wrongly considered that the reserve assets of the Nine were larger than was necessary and that therefore only three-fifths of these reserves should be pooled with the European Monetary Fund! He did, however, make a very important technical contribution to the mechanism of exchange-rate intervention, and it is a pity that this advice was not heeded during the recent international monetary débâcle. Mundell suggested a choice between two systems, the 'constrained' system and the 'permissive' system. According to the first one, the central agency would sell national currencies when the Europa was weak and the central banks would sell Europas when the national currencies were weak. Under the second system, national banks would support the Europa when it was weak (against a particular national currency) and the central agency would support a national currency when it was weak. Mundell favoured the 'permissive' system because he considered it to be foolproof against the speculators. However, as a word of warning, he suggested that the competent authorities would first have to agree on a set of basic rules, especially regarding overdrafts. Having accepted this important reservation, the author agrees strongly with Mundell's support for the 'permissive' system because, given an acceptable exchange rate for a currency, the central agency would throw all its resources behind one national currency and would defeat the speculators. Indeed, it would also be an economical way of conducting the exercise.

In the same publication, a number of other economists made observations about the use of the 'Europa'. Thus Meade, while supporting its denomination as a mixed bag of currencies, uttered words of caution. He saw dangers in the premature introduction of this unit of account because if it was not strong, a flight into national currencies might take place; therefore he suggested an initial 'official' use of large blocs of Europas. Equally, he stressed the necessity of making basic rules for the Monetary Fund. Lastly he uttered a word of caution about too great an emphasis on regional aid, pointing out that this was no panacea for economic co-ordination.

Neubauer went even further than Meade. He feared that the whole enterprise of economic and monetary union would fall into discredit unless more economic co-ordination was undertaken, and he stressed that the narrowing of the band round the currency parities (the 'Snake') made such co-ordination much more imperative than had previously been the case. Similarly, echoing somewhat Mundell's warning, he pointed out that an over-liberal policy by central banks (through their use of the European Monetary Fund) could discredit the Fund. This warning was nevertheless somewhat contradicted by his desire for greater independence for national central banks. Finally Neubauer favoured a harmonisation of monetary and credit policy and a freeing of capital movements. On this last point he did however agree that in recent years such movements have had only a limited efficacy.

Peeters differed from Meade in that he feared exactly the opposite development regarding the use of the Europas. He feared a manifestation of Gresham's Law whereby the Europas would become over-attractive and would, like gold, be kept in the reserves of central banks – pushing out less attractive national currencies for daily use.

In the same year the Commission[6] made a number

of proposals for the gradual pooling of national reserves over a number of years. These proposals were not accepted by the Council of Ministers. Two years later, in November 1975[7], a group of economists made proposals for an inflation-proof Europa which would be a European money of constant purchasing power. They suggested that the exchange-rate between the Europa and each of the national currencies should be adjusted by a weighted average of inflation rates of consumer prices expressed in national currencies. Initially, the Europa would be issued against equivalent amounts of national currencies so as not to increase the total monetary stock. Only at a later date would the Europa be issued through the rediscounting of bills and loans to the banking system.

The author's conclusions regarding the Europa are that there is little dissent about its composition but remarkable differences of opinion about its introduction and use. At the outset, we observe that the unit of account already exists and had even existed before its official creation, since the commercial banks already used such a unit in order to hedge their losses. This experience appears to lend slightly more credence to the thesis of Peeters than to those of Meade and Neubauer concerning the Europa. The fact is that Community loans denominated in this unit of account and backed by the E.E.C. are foolproof and very attractive. This is the way to make economic and monetary union work. Further, the financial work of the Community is conducted through the use of Europas – as Magnifico and Williamson suggested. Because of its attractiveness (not least as a hedge against inflation) it is likely to be used more and more. The use of the Europa does not, then, present any fundamental problem. The use of the European Monetary Fund and the problem of structural reform (economic co-ordination) are, alas, quite different matters.

The author, as a convinced European, would support at least a partial pooling of reserves in the European Monetary Fund. However, as Mundell has suggested, basic rules must be laid down for exchange-rate intervention. Nations must not be allowed to maintain perpetual balance of payments deficits. In exchange for such help they should be persuaded to undertake the necessary structural reform – possibly with the aid of the Community organs.

In conclusion, as Neubauer has correctly warned, inadequate preparation and economic co-ordination will inevitably discredit the whole enterprise of economic and monetary union. Thus those countries whose economies are most co-ordinated (the Five, for example) will be more likely to move swiftly towards such a union, thus providing a zone of monetary stability. In the case of other member states of the European Economic Community – which would seem to be more technically eligible for re-entry into the process of economic and monetary union – the possibility of maintaining a wider band than the existing 'Snake' should be examined. Thus the existing 'Snake' would continue in the case of the Five, but it might again move in a wide tunnel, henceforth composed of the currencies of other eligible member states.

Such a proposal seems to have found a partial echo

in the suggestions made in London, in June 1976, by the Dutch Treasurer-General, Mr Oort. The main point of reference for these proposals was the agreement in principle, by the I.M.F., on a set of rules for floating. Mr Oort suggested that the European Economic Community should itself adopt a similar set of rules, placing special emphasis on the principle of 'target zones' for exchange rates. Such zones should be periodically reviewed, probably every six months. The Treasurer-General admitted that the real problem here would be that of finding an 'appropriate objective indicator to trigger the adjustment'. He also saw the proposals as being in reality a form of 'crawling peg' system. One point which Mr Oort suggested – and which may unfortunately tend to be overlooked – is a call for some form of monetary discipline. The author would tend to underline this suggestion, since without this it is difficult to see how any form of economic welfare – let alone an economic and monetary union – can be achieved.

At about the same time as Mr. Oort was making his proposals the Dutch Finance Minister, Professor Duisenberg, was calling for a greater degree of economic and monetary co-ordination among the member states of the E.E.C. as a means of achieving an economic and monetary union.

5 Europe and Money: the Future

At the beginning of this study the observation was made that different European countries were in the process of re-examining their national economic and monetary philosophy and management. It was also suggested that Europe found itself presented with the golden opportunity of re-examining the basic principles of economic integration. One might go even further and suggest that we are before the most exciting and profound changes in economic thinking and management for at least half a century.

Here, a further observation should be made in addition to those made earlier. Although a number of member states of the European Economic Community might be said to constitute an optimum currency area, at least three countries (notably Britain, France and Italy) are persisting in their policy of seeking financial assistance for purposes of current internal consumption. This marks a profound and dangerous contrast with the period which existed before 1913, when financial help, if required, was necessitated by over-investment. The present situation suggests that a more serious readjustment of economic and monetary policy may be required than was originally presupposed. This also suggests that more effective means of controlling the monetary supply should be found. In turn this would seem to imply that some form of international discipline – somewhat along the lines suggested by Rueff[1] – might be necessary. This necessity is underlined by the persistence of some nations in borrowing from abroad, simply to finance consumption. Again this development gives weight to the desirability of re-examining the basic principles of the theory of economic integration.

Hitherto economists have been concerned with two major considerations when examining the theory of economic integration. First, they have been concerned with the optimisation of production through facilitating the free movement of the factors of production. Second, and this is the automatic counterpart to the former, they have been concerned with widening the choice of goods and services – available at the lowest possible prices – for the consumer.

To most economists the attainment of these goals implies an increase in welfare. There have, of course, been some voices which have queried this simplistic view – among these, that of Meade[2] has been one of the most important. Yet two very crucial considerations seem not to have received the degree of attention that they deserve. These are unemployment, caused by the removal of tariff barriers, and basic monetary policy.

The first-mentioned problem is one which has

already been experienced among some Common Market countries. In boom times one could expect a movement of workers between industries, leading to an absorption of redundant labour by growth centres. However in times of recession, such as at the time of writing, the tendency is for redundant or temporarily unemployed workers to remain without work. Paradoxically the situation does not remain as static as might be expected – in fact a loose international monetary policy allows deficit countries (where many workers may be unemployed) to import consumption goods from the surplus country. This policy does not solve anything – rather it tends to exacerbate an already untenable situation. What, then, should be done? Where has the theory of economic integration gone wrong? What might be the future for Europe and money?

It is possible that, with the notable exceptions of Balassa and Scitovsky,[3] most economists were in fact thinking in terms of boom and expansion when formulating theories of economic integration. It is true that most of the economists, whose work was examined above, were writing at a time when Western Europe, having experienced an explosion of population, was also enjoying economic expansion.

Today, unfortunately, this extraordinary population explosion is precisely one of our main economic problems. Also, during the years 1970–3, especially in the case of the United Kingdom, some countries were embarking upon a loose monetary policy. More recently this lack of monetary discipline has tended to receive the attention it rightly deserves.

Thus at this point one might conclude that both economists and governments have, on the whole, been living with and applying out of date theories. In many cases they have also failed to understand that things have radically changed since the energy crisis and the signing of the Lomé Agreement. The future of Europe and money is more circumscribed than might originally have been thought possible, and one can with a large degree of safety make the following prognosis.

A complete economic and monetary union in a customs union implies the absolute removal of all obstacles to the movement of the factors of production – plus the adoption of common economic and monetary policies. Naturally such a union can only voluntarily be accepted in times of economic expansion. In the immediate future, however, such expansion is likely to be only modest. This could imply, as has already been suggested, that some members of the European Economic Community will move ahead to a more advanced stage of economic and monetary union while others may opt for something half way between a free trade area and a customs union. These are distinct possibilities of which Europeans should be aware.

A further factor likely to influence Europe's role as a great international centre of investment is floating exchange rates. This factor, excluding any desires which some countries may express regarding the maintenance of their consumption of imports at present levels, is likely to diminish Europe's traditional role as an international investor because some countries whose currencies have been heavily devalued (notably France, Italy and the United Kingdom) present golden opportunities for foreign investors. Naturally such a situation does not exclude the recycling of funds by established European centres.

Signs are already evident that a number of member states of the European Economic Community are applying more vigorous incomes and monetary policies. Indeed, had they not done so on a relatively voluntary basis it is highly probable that their international creditors would have demanded the adoption of such policies. In turn, this does imply that the monetary policies of the different member states of the Common Market are likely to converge – out of sheer necessity. Such a development means that an important element of economic and monetary union will be adopted, almost by stealth.

None of these considerations will be likely to change the role of the European Economic Community as the world's greatest trading bloc. The Community is being courted by many countries – all wishing to sign trade agreements with Western Europe.[5] Also, the Common Market is the chief negotiator at international trade negotiations. These facts, to which should be added the recent increase in trade in more technically sophisticated products between the Community and the oil-producing states, imply both that the Community's trading status will be enhanced and that when the present recession is over and stable exchange rates are restored, Western Europe may well once more regain its place as a major international source of capital. Thus the long-term prospectives are positive: the immediate prospective regarding the theory of economic integration is less rosy, and yet very straightforward.

Quite simply, as is in fact being experienced, some member states of the European Economic Community, having long since discouraged the free flow of capital between themselves, now temporarily seek to reimpose the barriers to the free movement of goods and labour.

This situation would seem to imply that if the Community wishes to survive as a customs union in which the factors of production and goods are allowed to circulate freely, then the weaker members will demand some form of compensation which will be more important than a weakly endowed regional fund. Eventually such compensation might take a centralised institutional form – such as a central investment/employment fund – which would help the weaker members to restructure their economies. The other alternative would be to move towards a freeing of the flow of the factors of production – which would lead to an even greater excess of concentration in Europe than already exists.

What is likely to happen in the foreseeable future is that the different parts of the European Economic Community will develop economically at different speeds. Thus a few countries may well achieve a full economic and monetary union long before the others are prepared for such an advanced degree of economic and monetary integration. None of these factors are likely to diminish Western Europe's pre-eminence as the world's greatest trading bloc.

Hitherto great stress has been placed on monetary considerations and the need for stability in this field. Since the author believes that a minimum of monetary stability is synonymous with welfare, he considers that this should be one of the main aims of the Common Market. Nevertheless in every society it is the general practice to give a much fuller picture of welfare. This should not present an insurmountable problem in the European Economic Community, where it should be possible to arrive at a generally acceptable concept of welfare embracing a satisfactory level of employment, monetary stability, a wide degree of consumer choice, equality, and a variety of different types of opportunity ranging from education to lack of noise and little material pollution. The problem of employment should be tackled both at national and Community levels. Here the author would repeat his suggestion for the creation of a central employment/investment agency,[6] which could finance selected projects which might range from the restoration of the centre of a historic city to the setting up of a food-processing plant in a market-gardening district. The emphasis would thus be on relatively labour-intensive projects and works which would improve the quality of life; such prestige projects as Concorde and the Amsterdam metro would be excluded.

Reference has already been made to the beginning of a convergence in monetary policy between the member states of the Common Market. Sooner or later this was inevitable, since the international creditors of the big consumer spenders would not finance the party for ever. The different countries are in the process of rediscovering monetary discipline and its application. Monetary stability would help to mitigate excessive wage claims and in turn dampen down inflation.

This brings us to one of the most important concepts in customs union theory – the widening of consumer choice. Despite the revival of a wave of protectionism in some West European countries, one can safely say that the consumer choice in goods is really very wide. But the author maintains that the same cannot be said about the choice of services. It should be repeated that the main reason for this restriction is the non-existence of both a European Company Law and a law harmonising banking practices. Drafts for such laws are now before the Council of Ministers and are likely to be approved in the foreseeable future. These laws will almost automatically lead to a greater interpenetration within the Common Market by European companies, banks and services – thus increasing the welfare of Europeans. The energetic supervision of the Commission should ensure that collusion and concentration are kept to a strict minimum.

The other factors which have been mentioned are somewhat more subjective and the support they receive varies from country to country. Nevertheless, in a democratic organisation such as the European Economic Community, the very basic goal one should seek to attain is equality of opportunity – particularly in the field of education. The Community might also begin to move more energetically along the road towards a better distribution of income. The Community has, it is true, made some progress in the field of achieving one of the goals laid down in the Treaty of Rome – equal pay. But in countries such as Italy and France the differences in incomes between rich and poor are flagrant and are reflected in the existence of large Communist parties in both these countries. Naturally, resistance among the upper-income groups is strong towards any redistribution of income; despite this resistance, the future of the Community as a democratic body depends on the achievement of just such equality and member states should use their economic power to bring about this much-needed change.

The following conclusions may be reached concerning the future of Europe in the field of money and welfare. The present and the immediate future are riddled with difficulties because great disparities exist between the different member states concerning the degree of inflation and equality. This implies that although there has been a noticeable increase in welfare among the former Six of the European Economic Community, as reflected in the level of economic prosperity, the widening of consumer choice and the free movement of individuals, disparities in income have remained (and in some cases actually widened) in France and Italy; and since the early seventies great disparities in the level of inflation have been observed among the Nine. There has also been a tendency for the gap in prosperity between the richer and the poorer regions of the Community to widen.

The longer-term prospects for the Common Market would seem to be more encouraging. As already mentioned, there are at last signs (especially in the United Kingdom) that monetary discipline has been rediscovered.

It will of course take time for the necessary convergence of monetary policy among the member states to materialise, but we are at least witnessing a beginning of this trend. This should lead to a desirable degree of social stability in the Community.

In the field of consumer welfare, the adoption of a European Company Law and the law concerning the harmonisation of banking practices should lead to a greater interpenetration of the market and an increase in consumer choice. This will be a major step forwards, because hitherto the field of services has been neglected in favour of the production and distribution of goods.

On balance, then, the longer-term future would seem to be more positive than negative. There still remains one blot on the landscape, which is the already-mentioned disparity in equality and incomes both within individual member states and between the different regions of the Community. The removal, at least partially, of such disparities should be one of the main goals of the Common Market during the present and the coming decade.

Notes

Chapter 1

1. A. Maddison, 'Growth and Fluctuations in the World Economy 1870–1960', *Banca Nazionale del Lavoro Quarterly Review* (1962); S. Kuznets, *The Economic Growth of Nations* (Belknap Press, 1972).
2. According to the findings published in the Cunliffe Report the gold standard system, in reality, functioned in the following manner. In the case of a balance of payments deficit there would be a loss of gold (money) and a consequent contraction in the supply of money leading to an increase in its price (the discount rate) which would encourage an inflow of gold. In turn, due to the necessity for businessmen to obtain ready cash, the prices of goods would tend to fall and exports would increase. The improvement in the balance of payments would lead to a reduction in the discount rate.
3. The American equivalent of a central bank was not created until 1913.
4. According to the League of Nations statistics, the gross long-term overseas investments of France, Germany and the United Kingdom amounted to the equivalent of $40·5 billion in 1913. (*Note:* here and throughout this book the term 'billion' denotes one thousand millions.)
5. M. de Cecco, *Money and Empire* (Blackwell, 1974).

Notes

6 It is only if we include the United Kingdom in our calculations (see the table on p. 21) that the Common Market just becomes a net exporter of capital.
7 P. Coffey, *The External Economic Relations of the E.E.C.* (Macmillan, 1976).

Chapter 2

1 Quoted from G. Hallett, *The Social Economy of West Germany* (Macmillan, 1973).
2 J. Viner, *The Customs Union Issue* (Carnegie Endowment for World Peace, 1950).
3 J. E. Meade, *The Theory of Customs Unions* (North-Holland, 1956).
4 R. G. Lipsey and K. J. Lancaster, 'The General Theory of Second Best', *Review of Economic Studies*, 24 i, no. 63 (1956–7).
5 H. G. Johnson, 'An Economic Theory of Protectionism, Tariff Bargaining, and the Formation of Customs Unions', *Journal of Political Economy*, 73 (1965).
6 T. Scitovsky, *Economic Theory and Western European Integration* (Allen & Unwin, 1958).
7 B. Balassa, *The Theory of Economic Integration* (Allen & Unwin, 1962; originally published by 1961).
8 C. A. Cooper and B. F. Massell, 'A New Look at Customs Union Theory', *Economic Journal*, 75 (1965).
9 M. B. Krauss, 'Customs Union Theory: Ten Years Later', *Journal of World Trade Law*, 6, no. 3 (1972).
10 P. Coffey and J. R. Presley, 'London and the Development of a European Capital Market', *Bankers' Magazine* (June 1971).
11 A. P. Jacquemin, 'Size Structure and Performance of the Largest European Firms', *Three Banks Review*, no. 102 (June 1974) and *Économie Industrielle Européenne* (Ed. Dunod, 1975).

Chapter 3

1. R. A. Mundell, 'A Theory of Optimum Currency Areas', *American Economic Review*, 51 (1961).
2. Peter Coffey, 'European Monetary Integration Re-visited', *Revista de direito e economia*, Coimbra, Portugal (June 1975).
3. R. I. McKinnon, 'Optimum Currency Areas', *American Economic Review*, 53 (1963).
4. P. B. Kenen, 'The Theory of Optimum Currency Areas', in R. A. Mundell and A. K. Swoboda, *Monetary Problems of the International Economy* (Chicago University Press, 1969).
5. F. Onida, *The Theory and Policy of Optimum Currency Areas and their Implications for the European Monetary Union* (Suerf, 1972); G. Magnifico, *European Monetary Unification* (Macmillan, 1973).
6. W. M. Corden, 'Monetary integration', *Essays in International Finance* (Princeton, 1972).
7. J. M. Fleming, 'On Exchange Rate Unification', *Economic Journal* (Sept. 1971).
8. G. Haberler, *A Survey of International Trade Theory* (International Finance Section, Princeton, 1961).
9. J. R. Presley and C. E. J. Dennis, *Currency Areas: Theory and Practice* (Macmillan, 1976).
10. Peter Coffey, *The World Monetary Crisis* (Macmillan, 1974).

Chapter 4

1. See P. Coffey and J. R. Presley, *European Monetary Integration*, Part Two (Macmillan, 1971).
2. See Peter Coffey, 'European Monetary Integration Re-visited', *Revista de direito e economia*, Coimbra, Portugal (June 1975).
3. Van Den Tempel Report (E.E.C. Commission, 1969).
4. Reprinted in G. Magnifico, *European Monetary Unification* (Macmillan, 1973).

5 *European Economic Integration and Monetary Unification* (E.E.C. Commission, 1973).
6 Examined in Peter Coffey, *The World Monetary Crisis* (Macmillan, 1974).
7 *The Economist*, 1 Nov. 1975.

Chapter 5

1 J. Rueff, *La Réforme du Système Monétaire International* (Librairie Plon, 1973).
2 J. E. Meade, *The Theory of Customs Union* (North-Holland, 1956).
3 J. Scitovsky, *Economic Theory and Western European Integration* (Allen and Unwin, 1958); B. Balassa, *The Theory of Economic Integration* (Allen & Unwin, 1962).
4 P. Coffey, 'La Livre Sterling n'est probablement pas sous-évaluée', *Le Monde*, 13 July 1976; W. Rees-Mogg, 'How a 9·4% Excess Money Supply gave Britain 9·4% Inflation', *The Times*, 13 July 1976.
5 P. Coffey, *The External Economic Relations of the E.E.C.* (Macmillan, 1976).
6 It will be argued that such a proposal is in conflict with the author's insistence on monetary stability; he would, however, finance such a fund through cuts in defence spending and the salaries of civil servants – two areas of questionable productive value. The task of the proposed fund would be completely different from the work undertaken by the European Investment Bank and the Social Fund.

Index

ACP countries, 21; *see also* Lomé, Agreement of
Agricultural sector, 16, 17, 19, 36, 43, 45, 53, 64
Amsterdam, University of, 7
Appreciation, *see* Revaluation
Australia, 15

Balance of payments, 21, 44, 57, 61
　deficit of, 21, 42, 48, 57, 58, 75, 87n
　surplus of, 21, 42, 48, 57, 87n
Balassa, B., 31, 32, 33, 36, 37, 79, 88n
Bank Act, Peel's (1844), 12, 13
Bank of England, 12
Banking legislation, 8, 70, 84, 86
Banking system, 27, 35, 74
　links with, 27
　control of, 27
Banque de France, 24
Baring crisis (1890), 23
Belgium, 39, 45, 52, 59
Benelux, 51
Bilateralism, 20
Brandt, W., 62
Britain, *see* United Kingdom
Byé, M., 32, 33

Capital
　inflow of, 12, 19, 20, 31, 49, 52, 65, 66
　outflow of, 12, 14, 17, 19, 49, 65, 81, 87n
Cecco, de, M., 18, 87n
Coffey, P., 88n, 89n, 90n
Colonialism, 15, 18
Common agricultural policy, 30, 36, 61, 63, 68
Common currency, 41, 45, 51
Community budget, 63, 64, 65, 67, 68
Community loans, 68, 69, 71, 74
Comparative advantages, 53
Compensation, 56, 82
Competition, 26, 28, 31, 34, 36, 37
Competition policy, 26, 38
'Complementarity', 35, 45, 53
Concentration, 32, 35, 37, 39, 40, 82, 84
　control of, 26, 36
Concorde, 83
Consumer choice, 78, 83, 84, 85, 86
Convertibility, 13, 16, 24, 41, 47
Corden, W. M., 42, 45, 47, 48, 89n
Corporation tax, 64, 66, 67
Cooper, C. A., 34, 37, 88n
'Crawling peg', system of, 76
Cunliffe committee, 13, 87n
Currencies, 43, 44, 59, 63, 69, 71, 72, 73

Index

Currencies – *cont*
  linking together of, 44, 47, 48, 51, 54, 55, 56, 58
Customs union, 27–34 *passim*, 47, 65, 80, 82, 84
  'trade creation' effect of, 28, 29, 35, 36, 39
  'trade diversion' effect of, 28, 35, 36, 39

Denmark, 51, 52, 53
Dennis, C. E. J., 42, 49, 89n
Depreciation, *see* Devaluation
Devaluation, 48, 57, 58, 81
Dosser, D., 67
Duisenberg, W., 76

Economic development, 46, 53, 60, 61
  level of, 11, 52, 58
Economic integration, 11, 19, 22, 25, 60, 77
  theory of, 7, 8, 27–40, 78, 79, 82
Economic and monetary union, 7, 8, 31, 33, 40–82 *passim*
Economies of scale, 31, 32, 33, 34
'Economists', School of, 61
EEC, *see* European Economic Community
Energy crisis, 20, 61, 62, 80
Energy production, 19, 20
England, *see* United Kingdom
Equality, principle of, 65, 83, 84, 85, 86
Equal pay, 26, 85
Eucken, W., 25
Euro-dollar market, 40
'Europa' the, 70, 71, 72, 73, 74
European Banking Law, 37, 38, 39
European capital market, 31, 32, 40, 47, 69
European Central Bank, 32, 70, 71
European Company Law, 8, 37, 38, 39, 84, 86
European Economic Community, 7, 8, 16, 20, 21, 25–84 *passim*
  external relations of, 22, 88n

European Employment Agency, 9, 82, 83
European Investment Agency, 9, 82, 83
European Investment Bank, 71, 90n
European Monetary Fund, 61, 70, 71, 73, 74
Exchange rate intervention, 63, 71, 75
  constrained system of, 72
  permissive system of, 72
Exchange rates
  fixed, 16, 18, 24, 34, 41, 42, 45–7, 50, 57, 61
  floating, 21, 32, 42, 43, 48, 51, 57, 59, 76, 80
  variations in, 44, 47, 48
  adjustment of, 59, 74, 76
Excise duties, 64, 65

Federal Reserve Fund, 24, 31, 33
Financial centres, 18
  Berlin, 13
  London, 13
  Paris, 13
Five, the, 51, 52, 53, 54, 56, 59, 62, 69, 75
Fleming, J. M., 42, 48, 89
Four, the, 52, 54, 55, 62, 69
France, 8, 14–17 *passim*, 23–7 *passim*, 39, 54, 55, 61, 81, 85, 87n
Frankfurt am Main, 56
Free trade, 11, 12, 14, 16, 21, 28
Free Trade Area, 8, 27, 80
Freiburg, School of, 25

GATT, 20
Gehrels, F., 29
German Historical School, 29
German Union, 56
Giersch, H., 70
Gold
  inflow of, 13, 87n
  outflow of, 13, 87n
Gold reserves, 13, 73
Gold standard, 12, 13, 16, 18, 87n
'Good Creditor Policy', 14
Gresham, Law of, 73

Index 93

Haberler, G., 49, 89n
Hallett, G., 88n
Harmonisation
  fiscal, 33, 41, 63, 64, 65, 66, 68
  social, 33, 41
  monetary, 8, 41, 70, 73
'Hot money', 53, 54, 57, 58, 63

IBRD, 20
IMF, 20, 21, 76
'Inbuilt' stabiliser, 67, 68
Income distribution, 85, 86
Income policy, 30, 65, 81
India, 13, 14
Inflation, 12, 42, 50, 52, 63, 74, 85
  imported, 48, 58
Inter-commodity substitution, 29
Inter-country substitution, 28
Inter-penetration, 8, 21, 37, 38, 40, 84, 86
Interest rate, 13, 49, 58
  war, 58
International Capital Flows, 12
International division of labour, 18, 19, 20
International investment, 14, 18, 19, 21, 23, 36, 80
Investment projects, 65, 83
Ireland, Republic of, 45, 54, 55, 56
Italy, 37, 38, 39, 54, 55, 56, 77, 81, 85
  southern part of, 60

Jacquemin, A. P., 39, 88n
Johnson, H. G., 30, 35, 36, 88n
'Juste retour', principle of, 63, 64

Kenen, P. B., 42, 45, 50, 89
Kennedy Round Negotiations, 36
Keynes, J. M., 14
  plan of, 24
Krauss, M. B., 35, 88n
Kuznets, S., 12, 87n

Lancaster, K. J., 29, 30, 88n
Latin America, 14
League of Nations, 23, 87n

Lender of last resort, 24, 63, 71
Lipsey, R. G., 29, 30, 88n
List, 12
Lomé, Agreement of, 21; see also ACP countries
Luxembourg, 21n, 45, 52, 53, 54

McKinnon, R. I., 42, 44, 47, 48, 50, 52, 89n
Maddison, A., 12, 87n
Magnifico, G., 42, 45, 46, 50, 55, 69, 70, 74, 89n
'Market swapping', 35, 37
Massell, B. F., 34, 37, 88n
Meade, J. E., 29, 30, 31, 70, 72, 73, 74, 78, 88n, 90n
Mergers, 32, 38
  inter-state, 32, 37, 40
Metro, 83
Migration, 36, 48, 52, 55
Mobility,
  capital, 36, 39, 43, 49, 59, 81
  factor, 32, 34, 35, 43, 45–7, 60, 78
  geographical, 45
  industrial, 45
  labour, 36, 39, 43, 45, 47, 49, 52, 53, 57, 59, 79
Monetarists, School of, 61
Monetary assistance, 19, 24, 61, 77
Monetary discipline, 8, 13, 58, 76, 79, 84, 86
Monetary policy, 7, 8, 71, 78, 79, 80, 81, 83, 86
Money illusion, 47, 58
'Moneyness', 44
Money supply, 13, 74, 78, 87n
Monnet, J., 26
Mueller-Armack, A., 25, 36
Multinationals, 37, 39
Mundell, R. A., 42–9 passim, 70, 71, 72, 73, 79, 89n

Neo-liberalism, 26
Netherlands, the, 24, 39, 45, 48, 51, 52, 53
Neubauer, W., 70, 73, 74, 75
Neumark Report, 65
New York crisis (1907), 23
Nine, the, 71, 85

Index

Ohlin, B., 32
Oil crisis, *see* Energy crisis
Oil-producing countries, 81
Onida, F., 42, 45, 46, 55, 89n
Oort, C. J., 75, 76
'Openness', 44, 47, 50, 51, 54, 56, 58, 60
Optimum currency areas, 56, 57, 58, 59, 62, 77
    theories of, 8, 41–50, 51, 54
Overseas Investments, 14, 17, 18
    creation of markets through, 15
    factors influencing, 14–18
    political nature of, 16, 17
    profitability of, 15

Peeters, T., 73, 75
Philip, A., 26, 33
Planning, French School of, 26, 27
Presley, J. R., 42, 49, 54, 88n, 89n
Prest, A. R., 65, 67
'Propensity to inflate', 46, 50, 59
Protectionism, 23, 35, 84
Prussia, 56
Pseudo union, 47

Rees-Mogg, W., 90n
Regional Fund, 64, 82
Regions, 42, 43
    disequilibria between, 33, 42, 44, 46, 51, 52, 67, 73
    single product, 45
Restricted origin, principle of, 65
Revaluation, 48, 52, 57, 58
Ricardo, D., 11
Rome, Treaty of, 25, 26, 30, 85
    Articles 85 and 86, 37, 40
Rueff, J., 78, 90n
Russia, loans to, 16, 17

Schneider, E., 25
Scitovsky, T., 31, 32, 33, 36, 37, 79, 88n, 90n
Second best, theory of, 30
Segré Report, 69
Selected destination, principle of, 65

Six, the, 39, 60, 61, 85
Smith, A., 11
Snake, the, 73, 75
Social Fund, 64, 68, 90n
Social justice, 67
Social Market Economy, German School of, 25, 26, 27
Specialisation, 31, 32, 33, 34, 35, 37
Spraos, Professor, 29
Stability, 24, 43, 44, 48, 58, 62, 75, 83, 84, 86, 90n
Standardisation, 31
State
    monopoly, 66
    ownership, 26
    planning, 26
Sterling balances, 54, 55, 56, 63
Supra-nationality, 31, 32, 68, 71

'Target zones', 76
Tariff, 34, 35
    level, 78
    removal, 36
    revenues, 30
Tempel, van den, Report, 89n
Third World, 19, 22
Tinbergen, J., 31, 36
Tindemans, L., 62
Trading partner, 44, 47, 50, 51, 55, 56, 58

Unemployment, 21, 31, 42, 48, 50, 78, 79, 83
United Kingdom, 11–24 *passim*, 36, 43, 45, 54–63 *passim*, 77, 79, 81, 86, 87n, 88n
United States, 13, 14, 18, 20, 29, 31, 36, 43, 49, 55, 68
Unit of account, 70, 72, 74
Uri, P., 26

Value-added tax, 33, 64, 65, 66, 67
VAT, see Value-added tax
Verdoorn, P. J., 36
Vertical integration, 65
Vinelle, de la, 36

Viner, J., 27, 28, 29, 31, 35, 36, 37, 88n

Werner Report, 61
West Germany, 11, 14, 17, 20, 23–7 *passim*, 39, 48, 51–6 *passim*, 61, 87n
White, Plan of, 24

Williamson, 70, 74
World Economic Order, 7, 11–22, 24
World Monetary Order, 7, 11–22, 24
World War
  First, 7, 11, 12, 14, 22, 23, 24
  Second, 14, 20, 24, 25, 27

LIBRARY OF DAVIDSON COLLEGE